ASK
Faith Questions
in a Skeptical Age

Leader Guide

Ask
Faith Questions in a Skeptical Age

Book
978-1-5018-0333-8
978-1-5018-0334-5 eBook

DVD
978-1-5018-0337-6

Leader Guide
978-1-5018-0335-2
978-1-5018-0336-9 eBook

For more information, visit AbingdonPress.com.

Also by Scott J. Jones

The Wesleyan Way: A Faith That Matters

The Future of The United Methodist Church:
Seven Vision Pathways (Ed. with Bruce Ough)

Staying at the Table: The Gift of Unity for United Methodists

The Evangelistic Love of God and Neighbor:
A Theology of Witness and Discipleship

United Methodist Doctrine: The Extreme Center

John Wesley's Conception and Use of Scripture

Scott J. Jones and Arthur D. Jones

ASK

Faith Questions
in a Skeptical Age

LEADER GUIDE
by Barbara Dick

Abingdon Press / Nashville

ASK:
FAITH QUESTIONS IN A SKEPTICAL AGE

Leader Guide by Barbara Dick

This book is printed on elemental, chlorine-free paper.
ISBN 978-1-50180-335-2

15 16 17 18 19 20 21 22 23 24—10 9 8 7 6 5 4 3 2 1
MANUFACTURED IN THE UNITED STATES OF AMERICA

Contents

Contents

To the Leader

Welcome! In this study, you have the opportunity to help a group of learners examine some of the questions that we all wrestle with in our life of faith. Through the biblical witness, teachings from trusted voices of the past, and the wisdom gained from experience, Scott J. Jones and Arthur D. Jones take us on a journey of discovery and understanding toward more faithful and fulfilled living.

Questions can be either stumbling blocks or opportunities in our faith journeys and our conversations with others. Sometimes questions make us uncomfortable. Consider how to create the kind of safe learning environment in which participants can share their experiences and feelings honestly, as well as listen to others with sensitivity.

Scripture tells us that where two or three are gathered together, we can be assured of the presence of the Holy Spirit, working in and through all those gathered. As you prepare to lead, pray for that presence and expect to experience it.

This eight-session study makes use of the following components:

- The study book, *Ask: Faith Questions in a Skeptical Age*, by Scott J. Jones and Arthur D. Jones;
- This leader guide;
- The video segments that accompany the study.

You'll see that in the videos, the discussion group gathers around a box containing images, words, and Scriptures to serve as prompts for their discussion. You may choose to follow their example in your group by preparing a box for that same purpose. Under "Special Preparation" in each session plan, you'll find suggestions for items to put in the box.

Participants in the study will also need Bibles, as well as either a paper journal or an electronic means of journaling, such as a tablet. If possible, notify those interested in the study before the first session. Arrange for them to get copies of the book so that they can read the Introduction and Chapter 1.

Using This Guide with Your Group

Because no two groups are alike, this guide has been designed to give you flexibility and choice in tailoring the sessions for your group. The session format is listed below. You may choose any or all of the activities, adapting them as you wish to meet the schedule and needs of your particular group.

Most session time will be too short to do all the activities. Select ahead of time which activities the group will do, for how long, and in what order. Depending on which activities you select, there may be special preparation needed. The guide alerts the leader to what is needed before the session.

Session Format

The questions addressed in the study vary widely in focus from week to week. The objective, however, is always the same: to consider our thoughts and responses to the questions, then to gather those thoughts so we can provide confident witness to our faith in the world. With this in mind, the study has been designed to offer a structured flow of discovery and to provide freedom in exploring the questions and our responses together.

Planning the Session

Session Goals
Biblical Foundation
Special Preparation

Getting Started

Opening Prayer
Opening Activity

Learning Together

Bible Study
Video Study and Discussion
Book Study and Discussion

Wrapping Up

Practice
Preparation
Closing Prayer

Helpful Hints

Preparing for the Session

- Pray for the leading of the Holy Spirit as you prepare for the study. Pray for discernment for yourself and for each member of the study group.
- Before each session, familiarize yourself with the content. Read the book chapter again.
- Choose the session elements you will use during the group session, including the specific discussion questions you plan to cover. Be prepared, however, to adjust the session as group members interact and as questions arise. Prepare carefully, but allow space for the Holy Spirit to move in and through the group members and through you as facilitator.

- If you plan to use video clips or music suggestions, obtain appropriate projection equipment and be sure to test it before the session.
- Prepare the space where the group will meet so it will enhance the learning process. Ideally, group members should be seated around a table or in a circle so that all can see one another. Movable chairs are best, because the group will often form pairs or small groups for discussion.
- Bring a supply of Bibles for those who forget to bring their own. A variety of translations can be helpful.
- For most sessions, you will also need an easel with paper and markers, a whiteboard and markers, or some other means of posting group questions and responses.

Shaping the Learning Environment

- Begin and end on time.
- Establish a welcoming space. Consider the room temperature, access to amenities, hospitality, outside noise, and privacy. Use a small cross or candle as a focal point for times of prayer.
- Create a climate of openness, encouraging group members to participate as they feel comfortable. As mentioned above, some participants may be uncomfortable or embarrassed as they discuss these questions. Be on the lookout for signs of discomfort in those who may be silent, and encourage them to express their thoughts and feelings honestly. Assure group members that it is always acceptable to pass on a question.
- Remember that some people will jump right in with answers and comments, while others will need time to process what is being discussed.
- If you notice that some group members seem never to be able to enter the conversation, ask them if they have thoughts to share. Give everyone a chance to talk, but keep the conversation

moving. Moderate to prevent a few individuals from doing all the talking.

- Make use of the exercises that invite sharing in pairs. Those who are reluctant to speak out in a group setting may be more comfortable sharing one-on-one and reporting back to the group. This can often be effective in helping people grow more comfortable sharing in the larger setting. It also helps to avoid the dominance of the group by one or two of the participants (including you!).
- If no one answers at first during discussions, do not be afraid of silence. Help the group become comfortable with waiting. If no one responds, try reframing the language of the question. If no responses are forthcoming, venture an answer yourself and ask for comments.
- Model openness as you share with the group. Group members will follow your example. If you limit your sharing to a surface level, others will follow suit.
- Encourage multiple answers or responses before moving on.
- Ask, "Why?" or "Why do you believe that?" or "Can you say more about that?" to help continue a discussion and give it greater depth.
- Affirm others' responses with comments such as "Great" or "Thanks" or "Good insight"—especially if it's the first time someone has spoken during the group session.
- Monitor your own contributions. If you are doing most of the talking, back off so that you do not train the group to listen rather than speak up.
- Remember that you do not have all the answers. Your job is to keep the discussion going and encourage participation.

Managing the Session

- Honor the time schedule. If a session is running longer than expected, get consensus from the group before continuing beyond the agreed-upon ending time.

- When someone arrives late or must leave early, pause the session briefly to welcome them or bid them farewell. Changes in the makeup of the group alter the dynamics of the discussion and need to be acknowledged.
- Involve group members in various aspects of the group session, such as saying prayers or reading the Scripture.
- As always, in discussions that may involve personal sharing, confidentiality is essential. Remind the group members at each session: confidentiality is crucial to the success of this study. Group members should never pass along stories that have been shared in the group.

1.
Can Only One Religion Be True?

Planning the Session

Session Goals

Through the conversations and activities connected with this session, group members should begin to:

- Reflect on biblical passages that are related to the nature of faith and religion;
- Assess their personal faith stories in relation to Christianity;
- Explore teachings and experiences on the nature and function of religion.
- Prepare your own answer to this week's question: Can one religion be true?

Biblical Foundation

Ask, and you will receive. (Matthew 7:7)

You are one body and one spirit, just as God also called you in one hope. There is one Lord, one faith, one baptism, one God and Father of all, who is over all, through all, and in all. (Ephesians 4:4-6)

Dear friends, let's love each other, because love is from God, and everyone who loves is born of God and knows God. The person who doesn't love does not know God, because God is love. (1 John 4:7-8)

Special Preparation

- If group members are not familiar with one another, make nametags available.
- If possible, in advance of the first session, ask participants to bring either a journal or an electronic means of journaling, such as a tablet. Provide writing paper and pens for those who may need them. Also have a variety of Bible versions available for those who do not bring one.
- Make sure all participants have a copy of the study book, *Ask*. Invite them to read the introduction and chapter 1 in advance of the first session. You also should read this material.
- On a large sheet of paper or a board, print "Religion is…" and "Spirituality is…" as the heads of two columns.
- Have available easel pads or whiteboard, blank paper or construction paper, and markers or crayons.
- In the box, have available a variety of index cards and pictures that echo the items used in the session video, such as: picture of a member of ISIS and a victim; text of 1 Corinthians 13:12; the word *Evangelism*; the question "Why am I a Christian?"

Remember that there are more activities than most groups will have time to complete. As leader, you'll want to go over the session in advance and select or adapt the activities you think will work best for your group in the time allotted. Consider your own responses to questions you will pose to the group.

Getting Started

Welcome

As participants arrive, welcome them to the study and invite them to make use of the available Bibles, if they did not bring one.

Opening Prayer

Gracious and loving God, as we begin this study, open us to your presence and fill us—our time, our conversations, our reflections, our doubts, and our fears—with the joy of exploration and the wisdom of your love. We gather in Jesus' name. Amen.

Opening Activity

When all participants have arrived, invite them to introduce themselves by name and to complete verbally one of the posted prompts: "Religion is…" or "Spirituality is…" Do not take notes during the introductions.

When everyone has responded to the prompts, post responses on the sheet (or whiteboard). Participants may repeat their original responses or add to them. Defining these two terms provides a foundation and starting place for the study.

Learning Together

Bible Study

Here are the Scriptures for this session:

- Ephesians 4:4-6 ("One Lord, one faith, one baptism")
- 1 John 4:7-8 ("God is love")
- 1 Corinthians 13:12 ("Now we see a reflection; then we will see face-to-face;" try to include the NRSV or KJV)

Use the following process to study these Scriptures:

Ask for volunteers who are willing to read aloud from a variety of Bible versions.

As each passage is read, invite the participants to engage in "active listening." Instruct them to

- Sit comfortably (with uncrossed legs, if possible);
- Breathe slowly and deeply (expanding the diaphragm, not raising the shoulders);
- Focus on the words in one of these ways: close eyes; focus on a candle, a cross, or another object; look directly at the person reading the passage;
- Pay attention to any words that strike a chord, either negative or positive.

If the passage is read more than once or from more than one translation, instruct the active listeners to shift their focus for the second reading. The second time the passage is read, they might consider doing the following:

- Note emotional responses to the passage;
- Imagine the sensory environment of the first hearers: What would the first hearers taste, smell, see, or feel as they listened? What would they be wearing?
- Note what the passage is asking. When we allow ourselves to be encountered by the biblical text, we may hear a call to action or prayer.

After each passage has been read and heard in this way, invite participants to share words that "jumped out at them," insights that were gained, information that was learned, and any call to action or prayer that was received.

Video Study and Discussion

After viewing the video, form groups of 3–4 and ask the groups to give reactions to these comments from the video:

- "It's not me trying to be right. It's me trying to be faithful."
- "Does this mean that my Jewish friend or Muslim friend is going to hell?"
- "This doesn't mean that Jesus isn't right... what it means is that God is outside of whatever box we put him in."
- "While there are competing claims... I would argue that there's much more that [religions] actually share in common."
- "Every religion has a piece of truth, because God has been working through everybody."

When the small groups have had some time to share, bring the entire group together and invite someone from each group to share highlights of the conversation.

Book Study and Discussion

What Is Religion?

In Chapter 1, the authors invite us to explore the fundamental nature and function of religion. Ask participants to review their responses to the opening questions you posted: "Religion is..." and "Spirituality is..." and to share with the group which of the definitions seems most correct or helpful and why.

What Is Religion For?

The section of the book called "The Functions of Religion" offers a variety of responses to the question of religion's purpose in our lives, including providing answers to fundamental questions, building common culture, and giving an account of ultimate reality. List these functions on newsprint, and invite participants to share other functions of religion in their lives.

Four Approaches

The authors explore four approaches to the truth of religion. Learning to appreciate and respect views that differ from ours helps us to strengthen our views and beliefs. Form four small groups and ask each group to prepare a defense of one of the approaches:

1. Relativism
2. Agnosticism
3. Atheism
4. Religion

Each group should choose a spokesperson for its assigned approach and report to the large group.

Invite the spokespersons for relativism and agnosticism to role-play a four-minute debate. The rest of the participants will decide which approach wins. The winner will then engage in a four-minute debate with the spokesperson for atheism. The winner of that round will engage in a four-minute debate with the spokesperson for religion.

How to View Other Religions

In this section of the book, the authors invite us to approach other religions with "love, respect, and curiosity." Ask participants to describe what that looks like in their own lives.

Ask for a volunteer to read the second paragraph of this section: "In our faith tradition, we start with belief in the prevenient grace... openness and curiosity." The authors suggest that we consider this question when dealing with people of other religions: "How is God's grace at work in this person's life and practice?" Invite participants to share ways they agree or disagree with this suggestion.

Ask for a volunteer to read the paragraphs of this section beginning: "C. S. Lewis, in the last book of the Chronicles of Narnia ... common areas of interest and concern where we can work together." Invite participants to share how this story relates to their understanding of other faiths, Islam in particular.

Wrapping Up

Practice

Ask participants to reflect on the session question: "Can only one religion be true?"

In pairs, have each participant, in turn, pose/answer the session question. Prompt pairs to switch roles when half the allotted time has passed. Those posing the question should engage in active listening, so they will be prepared to share what they have heard when the group gathers again.

After all participants have had an opportunity to ask and answer the question, gather the group and invite people to share what they heard.

Preparation

Remind participants to read the next chapter and record questions and insights in their journals.

Closing Prayer

God of truth and grace, thank you for this time to reflect and learn about your truth. As we leave this place of learning and sharing, open our hearts and minds, that we might share your truth with the world. Amen.

Wrapping Up

Practice

Ask participants to reflect on the session question: "Can our world
be able to trust?"

In pairs, have each participant, in turn, pray/answer the session
question. Prompt pastor as/not reservation half the floor and studies
ponce. Those posing the question should engage in active listening so
they will be prepared to share what they have heard when the group
gathers again.

After all participants have had an opportunity to ask and answer
the question, gather the group and invite people to share what they
heard.

Preparation

Remind participants to read the next chapter and record questions
and insights in their journals.

Closing Prayer

God of truth and grace, thank you for praying for truth and grace about
your truth. As we know this place of knowing and sharing, open our
hearts and minds that we might share more fully from the truth begun.

2.
Why Is There Suffering and Evil?

Planning the Session

Session Goals

Through the conversations and activities connected with this session, group members should begin to:

- Reflect on biblical passages related to suffering and evil;
- Assess the role of suffering in their personal faith stories;
- Explore teachings and experiences on the nature and role of suffering and evil in the life of faith.
- Prepare an answer to the question: Why is there suffering and evil?

Biblical Foundation

God saw everything he had made: it was supremely good.... On the sixth day God completed all the work that he had done, and on the seventh day God rested from all the work that he had done. (Genesis 1:31, 2:2)

Now we see a reflection in a mirror; then we will see face-to-face. Now I know partially, but then I will know completely in the same way that I have been completely known. (1 Corinthians 13:12)

Special Preparation

- Invite the participants to read book Chapter 2 in advance of the session.
- In the box, have available a variety of index cards and pictures that echo the items used in the session video, such as: the word *Money*; the words *Natural disaster (volcanic eruption, flood, earthquake)*; the quotation "We know that the whole creation is groaning together and suffering labor pains up until now" (Romans 8:22); the words of the Wesley Covenant Prayer; the phrase *Free will*;

Getting Started

Welcome

As participants arrive, welcome them to the study and invite them to make use of the available Bibles, if they did not bring one.

Opening Prayer

Gracious God, we have all suffered. Help us to share with love and learn of your grace through our experiences and our sharing. Amen.

Opening Activity

When all participants have arrived, invite them to introduce themselves to each other by name and to share a time of suffering that caused them to wrestle with faith. This may be something in their lives or the lives of others. Be prepared for a variety of responses, including no response.

Do not take notes during the introductions. When participants have finished, ask them how it felt to share their struggles with faith.

- Encourage the participants to discuss one new insight from their journals.

Learning Together

Bible Study

Here are the Scriptures for this session:

- Genesis 1:31, 2:2 (Creation is very good; God rests)
- Romans 8:22 (Whole creation groaning in labor)
- Psalm 51 (Petition for forgiveness; be sure to include NRSV, KJV, NIV)
- John 9:1-7 (Jesus' response to the man blind from birth)

Use the same process as before to study these Scriptures:

Ask for volunteers to read aloud from a variety of Bible versions.

As each passage is read, invite the participants to engage in "active listening." Instruct them to

- Sit comfortably (with uncrossed legs, if possible);
- Breathe slowly and deeply (expanding the diaphragm, not raising the shoulders);
- Focus on the words in one of these ways: close eyes; focus on a candle, a cross, or another object; look directly at the reader;
- Note any words that strike a chord, negative or positive.

If the passage is read more than once or from more than one translation, instruct the active listeners to shift their focus for the second reading. They might

- Note emotional responses to the passage;
- Imagine the sensory environment of the first hearers: What would the first hearers taste, smell, see, or feel as they listened? What would they be wearing?
- Note what the passage asks. When we allow ourselves to be encountered by biblical text, we may hear a call to action or prayer.

After each passage has been read and heard in this way, invite participants to share words that "jumped out at them," insights gained, information learned, and any call to action or prayer received.

Video Study and Discussion

After viewing the video, form groups of 3–4 and ask the groups to give reactions to these comments from the video:

- "Whenever we offer simple answers to complicated questions, we do a disservice to people's faith."
- "There is nothing broken that God can't redeem."
- "God self-limits in order to allow us self-expression."
- "Whenever we try and speak on behalf of God, we begin to get outside of our pay grade."
- "'I don't know' is one of the best things we can say when we walk with people through what feels like hell on earth."
- "There's a really powerful thing that happens when we respond to evil with love."

When the small groups have had some time to share, bring the entire group together and invite someone from each group to share highlights of the conversation.

Book Study and Discussion

Ask participants to review the stories at the beginning of Chapter 2, where the authors share a variety of stories and events—war, terrorism, illness, natural disaster, human weakness, and sheer evil—that have led people to ask why God allows these things to happen.

The authors offer several responses to this question as it relates to natural disasters, disease, and human evil:

- The disobedience of Adam and Eve (original sin)
- The complexity of creation
- Free will

Form three small groups and assign one of the above explanations to each group to explore in more detail. Provide newsprint and markers to each group and ask them to review the chapter and their notes and to prepare a presentation that answers this question: In what ways and to what degree does this explanation account for the existence of natural disasters, disease, and human evil? Assure the groups that it is fine to conclude that the explanation is inadequate to account for these things. In that case, the group should present its process for reaching that conclusion.

When the small groups have had time to work, invite them to offer their presentations to the group.

Suffering Redeemed

Remind the group that sometimes, in an effort to offer comfort, people make statements about God's role in human suffering. The statements might include:

- God causes suffering as a means to test our faith.
- It is God's will that some people will suffer.
- Some people are not healed because they didn't pray hard enough.

Ask participants if they have heard or made statements such as these in times of suffering. Now read the authors' statements:

- "Suffering provides an opportunity for God's grace to be at work."
- "The Christian perspective is to help people experience the presence and love of Christ, even in the most difficult situations."

Facilitate a discussion of the way the authors' statements agree or disagree with the "words of comfort" sometimes offered. Invite participants to share new insights about the role of God's grace in framing a Christian response to suffering.

Wrapping Up

Practice

Ask participants to reflect on the session question: "Why is there suffering and evil?"

In pairs, have each participant, in turn, pose/answer the session question. Prompt pairs to switch roles when half the allotted time has passed. Those posing the question should engage in active listening, to be prepared to share what they have heard when the group regathers.

After all participants have had an opportunity to ask and answer the question, gather the group and invite people to share what they heard.

Preparation

Remind participants to read the next chapter and record questions and insights in their journals.

Closing Prayer

Great and good God, thank you for time to consider the ways that suffering and evil influence our life of faith. Continue to be with us as we journey together, to help us remember and praise your unconditional love and grace at work in the world. Amen.

3.

How Can I Believe in Science and Creation?

Planning the Session

Session Goals

Through the conversations and activities connected with this session, group members should begin to:

- Reflect on a biblical passage related to creation;
- Assess the role of science and biblical truth in their personal faith stories;
- Explore teachings and experiences on the nature and role of science in the life of faith.
- Prepare an answer to the question: How can I believe in science and creation?

Biblical Foundation

When God began to create the heavens and the earth—the earth was without shape or form, it was dark over the deep sea, and God's wind swept over the waters—God said, "Let there be light." And so light appeared. God saw how good the light was. God separated the light from the darkness. God named the light Day and the darkness Night. There was evening and there was morning: the first day. (Genesis 1:1-5)

Special Preparation

- Invite participants to read Chapter 3 in advance of the session.
- In the box, have available a variety of index cards and pictures that echo the items used in the session video, such as: image of the Tarantula Nebula; artwork of Adam and Eve in the garden of Eden; photo of Darwin's book *The Origin of Species*; photo of a Bible.

Getting Started

Welcome

As participants arrive, welcome them to the study and invite them to make use of the available Bibles, if they did not bring one.

Opening Prayer

Gracious and loving God, as we share our reflections and learning in this time and place, help us to remember that you are the source of all the knowledge and all the faith in our lives. We pray that this time together leads us to more faithful stewardship of your gifts. Amen.

Opening Activity

When all participants have arrived, invite them to introduce themselves by name and to share any thoughts they have about the role of science in their lives. Do not take notes during the introductions.

- Encourage participants to share one new insight from their journals.

Learning Together

Bible Study

Here is the Scripture for this session:

- Genesis 1:1-5 ("When God began to create . . ."; try to include NRSV, NIV, or KJV)

Use the same process as before to study these Scriptures:

Ask for volunteers to read aloud from a variety of Bible versions. As each passage is read, invite the participants to engage in "active listening." Instruct them to

- Sit comfortably (with uncrossed legs, if possible);
- Breathe slowly and deeply (expanding the diaphragm, not raising the shoulders);
- Focus on the words in one of these ways: close eyes; focus on a candle, a cross, or another object; look directly at the person reading the passage;
- Pay attention to any words that strike a chord, either negative or positive.

If the passage is read more than once or from more than one translation, instruct the active listeners to shift their focus for the second reading. They might

- Note emotional responses to the passage;
- Imagine the sensory environment of the first hearers: What would the first hearers taste, smell, see, or feel as they listened? What would they be wearing?
- Note what the passage is asking. When we allow ourselves to be encountered by the biblical text, we may hear a call to action or prayer.

After each passage has been read and heard in this way, invite participants to share words that "jumped out at them," insights gained, information learned, and any call to action or prayer received.

Video Study and Discussion

After viewing the video, form groups of 3–4 and ask the groups to give reactions to these comments from the video:

- "One of the most challenging things about reading Scripture is that we don't just read it; it reads us."
- "Truth includes facts, but it goes deeper and broader than the facts."
- "There's truth in both [religion and science], and they're actually asking different questions."
- "At the bottom of both science and faith is that mystery."
- "The Bible was not meant to be a scientific textbook."
- "You need more than facts to get to wisdom."

When the small groups have had some time to share, bring the entire group together and invite someone from each group to share highlights of the conversation.

Book Study and Discussion

In the section called "A Christian Answer," ask for a volunteer to read the next-to-last paragraph: "In other words, Scripture contains 'all things necessary' ... science and religion lead us toward different kinds of truth." Invite participants to share in what ways they agree or disagree with these statements.

Form three small groups and distribute newsprint and markers. Assign each group one of the following sections of the study text:

- Origin of the Cosmos
- Sustaining of the Universe
- Creation and Development of Life

Ask each group to review its assigned section as well as the section, "Wisdom in Both." The group should then prepare a presentation of the ways that both science and religion help us to understand the topic. After the small groups have had time to work, invite them to share presentations with the larger group.

Wrapping Up

Practice

Ask participants to reflect on the session question: "How can I believe in science and creation?"

In pairs, have each participant, in turn, pose/answer the session question. Prompt pairs to switch roles when half of the allotted time has passed. Those posing the question should engage in active listening, to be prepared to share what they have heard when the group gathers again.

After all participants have had an opportunity to ask and answer the question, gather the group and invite people to share what they heard.

Preparation

Remind participants to read the next chapter and record questions and insights in their journals.

Closing Prayer

God of eternity and time, we praise you for the goodness and beauty of creation. Help us to celebrate both mystery and knowledge in our faith journeys. Amen.

Wrapping Up

Practice

Ask participants to reflect on the seeking question, "How can I believe in science and creation?"

In pairs, have each participant, in turn, post-answer the session question. Prompt pairs to switch roles about half of the allotted time has passed. Those posing the question should engage in active listening to be prepared to share what they have heard when the group gathers again.

After all participants have had an opportunity to ask and answer the question, gather the group and invite people to share what they heard.

Preparation

Remind participants to read the next chapter and related questions and prepare to discuss them.

Closing Prayer

God of eternity and time, we thank you for this good time spent together. Help us to celebrate both reason and knowledge in our faith journeys. Amen.

4.
How Can I Believe
in a God I Can't Prove?

Planning the Session

Session Goals

Through the conversations and activities connected with this session, group members should begin to:

- Reflect on a biblical passage related to faith;
- Assess the role of experience and knowledge in their personal faith stories;
- Explore teachings and experiences on the existence of God.
- Prepare an answer to the question: How can I believe in a God I can't prove?

Biblical Foundation

Faith is the reality of what we hope for, the proof of what we don't see. (Hebrews 11:1)

Special Preparation

- Invite participants to read Chapter 4 in advance of the session.

- In a box, have available index cards and pictures that echo the items used in the session video, such as: the Stephen Hawking quotation "Before we understand science, it is natural to believe that God created the universe. But now science offers a more convincing explanation."; the question "Did humans invent God?"

Getting Started

Welcome

As participants arrive, welcome them to the study and invite them to make use of the available Bibles, if they did not bring one.

Opening Prayer

God of love, we walk by faith. We pray that this time of sharing and learning moves us to deeper certainty in our lives and deeper confidence in our words as we share our faith with others. In the name of Jesus the Christ, we pray. Amen.

Opening Activity

When all participants have arrived, invite them to introduce themselves by name and to share what faith means to them. Do not take notes during the introductions.

- Encourage participants to share insights from their journals.

Learning Together

Bible Study

Here is the Scripture for this session:

- Hebrews 11:1 ("Faith is ...;" try to include KJV, NRSV, NIV)

Use the same process as before to study these Scriptures:

Ask for volunteers to read aloud from a variety of Bible versions. As each passage is read, invite the participants to

- Sit comfortably (with uncrossed legs, if possible);
- Breathe slowly and deeply (expanding the diaphragm, not raising the shoulders);
- Focus on the words in one of these ways: close eyes; focus on a candle, a cross, or another object; look directly at the reader;
- Pay attention to any words that strike a chord, either negative or positive.

If the passage is read more than once or from more than one translation, instruct the active listeners to shift their focus for the second reading. They might

- Note emotional responses to the passage;
- Imagine the sensory environment of the first hearers: What would the first hearers taste, smell, see, or feel as they listened? What would they be wearing?
- Note what the passage is asking. When we allow ourselves to be encountered by the biblical text, we may hear a call to action or prayer.

After each passage has been read and heard in this way, invite participants to share words that "jumped out at them," insights gained, information learned, and any call to action or prayer received.

Video Study and Discussion

After viewing the video, form groups of 3–4 and ask the groups to give reactions to these comments from the video:

- "If we could prove God, then we would be God."
- "Waiting for proof is agnosticism."

- "I would never want people to think that you have to check your brain at the door."
- "Doubt is not the enemy of faith. It can be a doorway that leads us closer to God."
- "Stop wrestling with those questions to the point of paralysis, and start serving."
- "If you really believe something, you're going to act on it."

When the small groups have had some time to share, bring the entire group together and invite someone from each group to share highlights of the conversation.

Book Study and Discussion

Does God Exist?

The authors point out that one's level of intelligence has no bearing on belief or behavior. Share their statement, "Both atheists and persons of faith have the capacity for greatness as well as depravity, and neither response has any effect on whether or not there is a God." Remind the group that the focus of this session is on the existence of God, not on the character of believers or nonbelievers.

Ask participants to respond to the question, "Do you believe that God exists? Why?" Invite group members to engage in respectful, active listening as each person shares. Remember, it is always acceptable for an individual to choose not to share.

Form three groups and ask each group to review the chapter and form a definition of one of the following positions on the existence of God:

- Theism
- Atheism
- Agnosticism

When the small groups have had time to work, invite them to share their definitions with the larger group.

Wrapping Up

Practice

Ask participants to reflect on the session question: "How can I believe in a God I can't prove?"

In pairs, have each participant, in turn, pose/answer the session question. Prompt pairs to switch roles when half of the allotted time has passed. Those posing the question should engage in active listening, to be prepared to share what they have heard when the group gathers again.

After all participants have had an opportunity to ask and answer the question, gather the group and invite people to share what they heard.

Preparation

Remind participants to read the next chapter and record questions and insights in their journals.

Closing Prayer

Come, Holy Spirit, come. Fill our lives with faith, hope, and trust. Help us learn to share the truth of our faith with those who long to know you. Let the power of your grace shine through the facts of our lives. Amen.

Wrapping Up

Practice

Ask participants to reflect on the session question: How can I believe in a God I can't prove?

In pairs, have each participant, in turn, pose/answer the session question. Partner pairs to switch roles when half of the allotted time has passed. Those posing the question should repeat it, actively listening to be prepared to share what they have heard when the group gathers again.

After all participants have had an opportunity to ask and answer the question, gather the group and invite people to share what they heard.

Preparation

Remind participants to read the next chapter and record questions and insights in their journals.

Closing Prayer

Come, Holy Spirit, fill us free with faith, hope, and trust. Help us turn to share the truth of your truth with those who long to know you. Let me power in your grace shine through the lens of our lives. Amen.

5.
Can I Trust the Old Testament?

Planning the Session

Session Goals

Through the conversations and activities connected with this session, group members should begin to:

- Reflect on biblical passages from the Old Testament and the New Testament;
- Assess the role of Old Testament truth in their personal faith stories;
- Explore Old Testament teachings and experiences that form a foundation for the life of faith.
- Prepare an answer to: Can I trust the Old Testament?

Biblical Foundation

Israel, listen! Our God is the LORD! Only the LORD! Love the LORD your God with all your heart, all your being, and all your strength. (Deuteronomy 6:4-5)

You must not take revenge nor hold a grudge against any of your people; instead, you must love your neighbor as yourself; I am the LORD. (Leviticus 19:18)

He replied, "You must love the Lord your God with all your heart, with all your being, and with all your mind. This is the first and greatest commandment. And the second is like it: You must love your neighbor as you love yourself. All the Law and the Prophets depend on these two commands." (Matthew 22:37-40)

Special Preparation

- Invite participants to read Chapter 5 in advance of the session.
- In the box, have available a variety of index cards and pictures that echo the items used in the session video, such as: the Scripture "I have loved you with an everlasting love" (Jeremiah 31:3 NRSV); picture of sacrifice of Jacob; the Scripture "Do not think that I have come to abolish the law or the prophets; I have come not to abolish but to fulfill" (Matthew 5:17 NRSV).

Getting Started

Welcome

As participants arrive, welcome them to the study and invite them to make use of the available Bibles, if they did not bring one.

Opening Prayer

One Lord, one faith—from creation through resurrection and into our lives of faith. Walk with us as we explore and learn together how the sacred texts work in unity to teach us your love. Amen.

Opening Activity

When all participants have arrived, invite them to introduce themselves by name and to share their favorite Old Testament story or quotation. Do not take notes during the introductions.

- Encourage participants to share an insight from their journals.

Learning Together

Bible Study

Here are the Scriptures for this session:

- Deuteronomy 6:4-5 (The Shema, "Hear, O Israel")
- Leviticus 19:18 ("Love your neighbor")
- Matthew 22:37-40 (Two great commandments)

Use the same process as before to study these Scriptures:

Ask for volunteers to read aloud from a variety of Bible versions. As each passage is read, invite the participants to engage in "active listening." Instruct them to

- Sit comfortably (with uncrossed legs, if possible);
- Breathe slowly and deeply (expanding the diaphragm, not raising the shoulders);
- Focus on the words in one of these ways: close eyes; focus on a candle, a cross, or another object; look directly at the reader;
- Pay attention to any words that strike a chord, either negative or positive.

If the passage is read more than once or from more than one translation, instruct the active listeners to shift their focus for the second reading. They might

- Note emotional responses to the passage;
- Imagine the sensory environment of the first hearers: What would the first hearers taste, smell, see, or feel as they listened? What would they be wearing?
- Note what the passage is asking. When we allow ourselves to be encountered by the biblical text, we may hear a call to action or prayer.

After each passage has been read and heard in this way, invite participants to share words that "jumped out at them," insights gained, information learned, and any call to action or prayer received.

Video Study and Discussion

After viewing the video, form groups of 3–4 and ask the groups to give reactions to these comments from the video:

- "How do we push past the isolated sound bite that's based on limited understanding?"
- "A lot of Christians say the Old Testament's hard; it's difficult; I don't want to mess with it."
- "The Old Testament stories help us to make sense of Jesus. They were the waters he was swimming in."
- "I trust the Old Testament, because in it I see my own struggles."
- "God's heart hasn't changed [since the time of the Old Testament], but maybe we as humans have changed."

When the small groups have had some time to share, bring the entire group together and invite someone from each group to share highlights of the conversation.

Book Study and Discussion

God in the Old Testament

Invite participants to share when/where/how they learned about the Bible. How familiar are they with the Old Testament?

Ask the group to review the section, "Difficult Passages in the Old Testament." Invite participants to share in what ways they agree or disagree with the authors' statement at the end of that section: "Such passages—depicting a God of war, violence, slavery, and scientific absurdities—are reasons why many readers are reluctant to trust the Old Testament."

Now ask for volunteers who would be willing to read the following passages from the Bible:

- Genesis 1:31 (Supremely good creation)
- Psalm 100 (Praise)
- Isaiah 2:4 ("Swords into iron plows")
- Isaiah 40:28-31 ("Haven't you heard?")
- Isaiah 65:17-25 (New heaven and new earth)
- Jeremiah 29:11 ("Future filled with hope")
- Jeremiah 31:33 (Instructions engraved on the heart)

Invite participants to share some ways in which these passages change or influence their understanding of God in the Old Testament. Invite them to name other Old Testament passages that have inspired them and taught them about God's love.

People in the Old Testament

Form groups of 3–4. Assign each group one of the following passages from the Bible. Ask each group to review the passage, consider it carefully, and then answer the following question: What does this passage teach us about God, about people, and about our relationship with God?

- Genesis 3 (Human temptation)
- Exodus 3 (Moses at the burning bush)
- Deuteronomy 10:12-22 ("Circumcise your hearts")
- Deuteronomy 30:11-20 ("Choose life")
- 1 Samuel 8 (The people demand a king)
- Jeremiah 29:1-14 (God's promise)
- Micah 6:6-8 ("What the Lord requires")

When the groups have had time to work, invite them to read the passage aloud and share their response to the question.

Wrapping Up

Practice

Ask participants to reflect on the session question: "Can I trust the Old Testament?"

In pairs, have each participant, in turn, pose/answer the session question. Prompt pairs to switch roles when half of the allotted time has passed. Those posing the question should engage in active listening, to be prepared to share what they have heard when the group gathers again.

After all participants have had an opportunity to ask and answer the question, gather the group and invite people to share what they heard.

Preparation

Remind participants to read the next chapter and record questions and insights in their journals.

Closing Prayer

God of Abram, of Sarai, of Isaiah, of Paul, of Lydia, help us to embrace the eternal truth of your Word, alive through the ages and alive today. May it live in us as we share our faith with others. Amen.

6.
Are Marriage, Sex, and Family Life Religious Issues?

Planning the Session

Session Goals

Through the conversations and activities connected with this session, group members should begin to:

- Reflect on biblical passages that are related to the subjects of sex and family life;
- Assess the role of sex and family life in their personal faith stories;
- Explore teachings and experiences on the function and role of sex and family in the life of faith.
- Prepare an answer to this week's question: Are marriage, sex, and family life religious issues?

Biblical Foundation

God blessed them and said to them, "Be fertile and multiply." (Genesis 1:28)

This is the reason that a man leaves his father and mother and embraces his wife, and they become one flesh. (Genesis 2:24)

45

Jesus said, "Neither do I condemn you. Go, and from now on, don't sin anymore." (John 8:11)

Special Preparation

- Invite participants to read Chapter 6 in advance of the session.
- In the box, have available a variety of index cards and pictures that echo the items used in the session video, such as: picture of a traditional wedding; the quotation "354 million people are viewing pornographic images online"; the word *Divorce*; a picture of long-time married couple; a picture of a *Cosmopolitan* magazine cover.

Getting Started

Welcome

As participants arrive, welcome them to the class and the study, and invite them to make use of the available Bibles, if they did not bring a Bible of their own.

Opening Prayer

God of good creation, as we share our questions and doubts, reveal to us the integrity and joy of living through love in all of our relationships. Amen.

Opening Activity

When all participants have arrived, invite them to introduce themselves by name and to describe briefly the family in which they grew up. Do not take notes during the introductions.

- Encourage participants to share one new insight from their journals.

Learning Together

Bible Study

Here are the Scriptures for this session:

- Genesis 1:28 ("Multiply")
- Genesis 2:24 ("Become one flesh")
- John 8:3-11 ("Go and sin no more")
- Exodus 20:12-17 (Honor your parents through do not covet; try to include NRSV, NIV, or KJV)

Use the same process as before to study these Scriptures:

Ask for volunteers to read aloud from a variety of Bible versions. As each passage is read, invite the participants to engage in "active listening." Instruct them to

- Sit comfortably (with uncrossed legs, if possible);
- Breathe slowly and deeply (expanding the diaphragm, not raising the shoulders);
- Focus on the words in one of these ways: close eyes; focus on a candle, a cross, or another object; look directly at the reader;
- Pay attention to any words that strike a chord, either negative or positive.

If the passage is read more than once or from more than one translation, instruct the active listeners to shift their focus for the second reading. They might

- Note emotional responses to the passage;
- Imagine the sensory environment of the first hearers: What would the first hearers taste, smell, see, or feel as they listened? What would they be wearing?

- Note what the passage is asking. When we allow ourselves to be encountered by the biblical text, we may hear a call to action or prayer.

After each passage has been read and heard in this way, invite participants to share words that "jumped out at them," insights gained, information learned, and any call to action or prayer received.

Video Study and Discussion

After viewing the video, form groups of 3–4 and ask the groups to give reactions to these comments from the video:

- "The church has lost its credibility as a community where we can have honest conversations about sex."
- "What a gift it is that God wants to be in that part of our lives."
- "The church has wonderful resources through the redemptive story of Christ to deal with the shame people are carrying around in their sexual lives."
- "We're called to make each other better. That's what marriage is fundamentally for me."

When the small groups have had some time to share, bring the entire group together and invite someone from each group to share highlights of the conversation.

Book Study and Discussion

Read this quotation that comes from the study book: "Does God really care what we do in our bedrooms?" Invite participants to respond and share the reasons for their responses.

Conflicting Statements

The authors explore several conflicting and seemingly contradictory perspectives on Scripture and sexuality. Form four small groups and assign to each group one pair of book quotations from the list below.

Ask the groups to prepare a list of questions for study or discussion on the assigned pair of quotations, using the text and their own knowledge and experience as resources.

1a. "The public perception about churches and sexuality is that religion exists to restrict sexual activity."	1b. "this first guideline about sex in Scripture is the exact opposite.... Instead of Don't do it! God says, Do it!"
2a. "Sex is not the primary topic of Scripture...."	2b. "the basic story of Scripture: that we are good but full of brokenness."
3a. "One of the goals for sex and marriage in Scripture is procreation."	3b. "not every married couple is able to or is called to procreate, but every couple is meant to grow in serving and loving God."
4a. "Our culture tells us that we are defined by our gender or sexuality."	4b. "the Christian story is that we are defined by God."

When the small groups have had time to work, gather the larger group and invite the small groups to present their questions and any possible answers that were mentioned in the process of writing them.

High Expectations ... High Grace

Share this quotation that comes from the study book: "When we fall short, we need both the high expectations and high grace." Invite participants to share if they agree with this statement. Ask what they think the authors mean by "high expectations" and "high grace."

Wrapping Up

Practice

Ask participants to reflect on the session question: "Are marriage, sex, and family life religious issues?"

In pairs, have each participant, in turn, pose/answer the session question. Prompt pairs to switch roles when half of the allotted time has passed. Those posing the question should engage in active listening, to be prepared to share what they have heard when the group gathers again.

After all participants have had an opportunity to ask and answer the question, gather the group and invite people to share what they heard.

Preparation

Remind participants to read the next chapter and record questions and insights in their journals.

Closing Prayer

Oh God, whose good creation we are, walk with us as we witness to lives of joy and integrity in our relationships with others and with you. Amen.

7.
Was Jesus' Resurrection Real?

Planning the Session

Session Goals

Through the conversations and activities connected with this session, group members should begin to:

- Reflect on biblical passages related to resurrection;
- Assess the role of the Resurrection in their faith stories;
- Explore teachings on and experiences of the Resurrection in the life of faith.
- Prepare an answer to the question: Was Jesus' resurrection real?

Biblical Foundation

> If Christ hadn't been raised, then your faith is worthless; you are still in your sins. (1 Corinthians 15:17)

Special Preparation

- Invite participants to read Chapter 7 in advance of the session.
- In the box, have available a variety of index cards and pictures that echo the items used in the session video, such as: picture of empty tomb; picture of Santa Claus; picture of Holy Communion; the equation "2+2=4"; the Scripture "Unless I see ... I won't believe" (John 20:25).

Getting Started

Welcome

As participants arrive, welcome them to the study and invite them to make use of the available Bibles, if they did not bring one.

Opening Prayer

Risen Christ, we gather today to deepen our understanding of your sacrificial love. Help our sharing and learning to transform us. Fill us with resurrection joy so that your love can shine through our lives. Amen.

Opening Activity

When all participants have arrived, invite them to introduce themselves by name and to share a favorite Easter memory. Do not take notes during the introductions.

- Encourage participants to share an insight from their journals.

Learning Together

Bible Study

Here are the Scriptures for this session:

- Luke 24:30-31; 38-43 (Jesus' resurrection body)
- John 20:26-29 (Believe without seeing)
- 1 Corinthians 15:17 ("If Christ hasn't been raised ...")
- 1 Corinthians 15:35-53 (Our resurrection bodies)

Use the same process as before to study these Scriptures:

Ask for volunteers to read aloud from a variety of Bible versions. As each passage is read, invite the participants to engage in "active listening." Instruct them to

- Sit comfortably (with uncrossed legs, if possible);
- Breathe slowly and deeply (expanding the diaphragm, not raising the shoulders);
- Focus on the words in one of these ways: close eyes; focus on a candle, a cross, or another object; look directly at the reader;
- Note any words that strike a chord, either negative or positive.

If the passage is read more than once or from more than one translation, instruct the active listeners to shift their focus for the second reading. They might

- Note emotional responses to the passage;
- Imagine the sensory environment of the first hearers: What would the first hearers taste, smell, see, or feel as they listened? What would they be wearing?
- Note what the passage is asking. When we allow ourselves to be encountered by the biblical text, we may hear a call to action or prayer.

After each passage has been read and heard in this way, invite participants to share words that "jumped out at them," insights gained, information learned, and any call to action or prayer received.

Video Study and Discussion

After viewing the video, form groups of 3–4 and ask the groups to give reactions to these comments from the video:

- "In the most painful moments of life, God will still have the last word somehow."
- "Treating Jesus as if he were alive instead of dead is the difference between a nominal faith and a faith that's on fire."
- "Christ becomes real in those moments we live through today."
- "God continues to work even beyond death; that's a hope that can change the way we live."

- "The disciples doubted the Resurrection, and every disciple since has doubted the Resurrection."
- "I see resurrection happening all the time in people's lives."

When the small groups have had some time to share, bring the entire group together and invite someone from each group to share highlights of the conversation.

Book Study and Discussion

Ask the participants to reflect on the Resurrection and their understanding of it fifteen years ago and today. Have their perceptions changed? Why and in what ways? After they have had some time to work, invite group members to share their thoughts and reflections.

Logical Possibilities

Form four small groups and assign each group one of the options covered in the section of the text called "Logical Possibilities." Ask each group to review the text and prepare to argue for the position assigned. Let them know they will have three minutes for their presentation, and they should be prepared to answer questions from the rest of the group.

> Jesus never existed.
> Jesus didn't die on the cross.
> Jesus died, but someone stole his body.
> Jesus' resurrection happened.

When the small groups have had time to work, invite each one in turn to take three minutes to make the case for their position. Then encourage the rest of the participants to ask questions about the position taken.

A Story with Consequence for Us

Read or have someone read these quotations that come from the study book:

- "C. S. Lewis put it this way: 'Christianity, if false, is of no importance, and if true, of infinite importance. The one thing it cannot be is moderately important.'"[1]
- "If scientific proof of Jesus' resurrection is unavailable, then why do so many believe?"
- "The Resurrection is of no value for our lives if it *might* be true."

Ask participants to share ways in which they agree or disagree with these statements.

Wrapping Up

Practice

Ask participants to reflect on the session question: "Was Jesus' resurrection real?"

In pairs, have each participant, in turn, pose/answer the session question. Prompt pairs to switch roles when half the allotted time has passed. Those posing the question should engage in active listening, to be prepared to share what they heard when the group gathers again.

After all participants have had an opportunity to ask and answer the question, gather the group and invite people to share what they heard.

Preparation

Remind participants to read the next chapter and record questions and insights in their journals.

Closing Prayer

Creator, Redeemer, Sustainer, open our hearts, our minds, our voices, to sing the glory of resurrection faith! We are changed by your Word! Use our words to bring the love of your Word to others. Amen.

---

1. C. S. Lewis, "Christian Apologetics," in *God in the Dock* (Grand Rapids: W. M. Eerdmans, 2014), 102.

8.
Why Do Christians Disagree About So Many Things?

Planning the Session

Session Goals

Through the conversations and activities connected with this session, group members should begin to:

- Reflect on biblical passages related to unity;
- Assess the importance of conscious choices they have made about essential doctrines in their personal faith stories;
- Explore teachings and experiences on unity and disunity in the life of faith.
- Prepare an answer to the question: Why do Christians disagree about so many things?

Biblical Foundation

"As you sent me into the world, so I have sent them into the world. I made myself holy on their behalf so that they also would be made holy in the truth.

"I'm not praying only for them but also for those who believe in me because of their word. I pray they will be one,

Father, just as are in me and I am in you. I pray that they also will be in us, so that the world will believe that you sent me. I've given them the glory that you gave me so that they can be one just as we are one. I'm in them and you are in me so that they will be made perfectly one. Then the world will know that you sent me and that you have loved them just as you loved me." (John 17:18-23)

Special Preparation

- Invite participants to read Chapter 8 in advance of the session.
- Post at the top of a sheet of newsprint or whiteboard: "In essentials, unity; in nonessentials, liberty; in all things, charity." Beneath the statement, write Essentials and Nonessentials as the heads of two columns.
- In the box, have available index cards and pictures that echo the items in the session video, such as: names of Jim Jones, Joseph Smith, Billy Graham, Jeremiah Wright, John Wesley, Martin Luther, Pope Francis; text of the Apostles' Creed; the word *Unity*; the following list: predestination, free will, infant baptism, ordination of women, sexuality, reproductive rights, capital punishment.

Getting Started

Welcome

As participants arrive, welcome them to the study and invite them to make use of the available Bibles, if they did not bring one.

Opening Prayer

Creator, Redeemer, Sustainer, Three in One, we gather here to confess our failure to live in unity. We seek to learn where love unites us and how to live in the light of that love. Amen.

Opening Activity

When all participants have arrived, invite them to introduce themselves by name and to share their definition of the word unity. Do not take notes during the introductions.

- Encourage participants to share one new insight from their journals.

Learning Together

Bible Study

Here are the Scriptures for this session:

- John 17:18-23 ("I pray they will be one")
- Ephesians 4:1-6 ("Preserve the unity of the Spirit")
- 2 Corinthians 5:19 (We have the message of reconciliation)
- Romans 12:9-21 ("Live at peace with all people") *Note:* Don't get hung up on the "pile burning coals on his head" of verse 20. In first-century Palestine, many things were carried on the head. This could include a brazier of burning coals to warm the house and cook food. In the context of providing food and drink for an enemy, this phrase emphasizes overcoming evil with good, with generosity. Consider mentioning this to the group before the passage is read.)

Use the same process as before to study these Scriptures:

Ask for volunteers to read aloud from a variety of Bible versions. As each passage is read, invite the participants to engage in "active listening." Instruct them to

- Sit comfortably (with uncrossed legs, if possible);
- Breathe slowly and deeply (expanding the diaphragm, not raising the shoulders);

- Focus on the words in one of these ways: close eyes; focus on a candle, a cross, or another object; look directly at the reader;
- Pay attention to any words that strike a chord, either negative or positive.

If the passage is read more than once or from more than one translation, instruct the active listeners to shift their focus for the second reading. They might

- Note emotional responses to the passage;
- Imagine the sensory environment of the first hearers: What would the first hearers taste, smell, see, or feel as they listened? What would they be wearing?
- Note what the passage is asking. When we are encountered by the biblical text, we may hear a call to action or prayer.

After each passage has been read and heard in this way, invite participants to share words that "jumped out at them," insights gained, information learned, and any call to action or prayer received.

Video Study and Discussion

After viewing the video, form groups of 3–4 and ask the groups to give reactions to these comments from the video:

- "All of us argue. Why should Christians be any different?"
- "When we gather together even in our disagreements, Christ is present."
- "How can we disagree well?"
- "It's our unity in Christ and God, not our unity in all opinions."
- "My favorite image of unity in the church is the picture of Holy Communion."
- "Iron sharpens iron—we need others to help us become who Christ wants us to be."

- "The truth of what God is trying to do is so big that we can't grasp it fully."

When the small groups have had some time to share, bring the entire group together and invite someone from each group to share highlights of the conversation.

Book Study and Discussion

If you have not already done so, post at the top of a sheet of newsprint or whiteboard: "In essentials, unity; in nonessentials, liberty; in all things, charity." Beneath the statement, write *Essentials* and *Nonessentials* as the heads of two columns. Inform the group that the statement will guide your discussion of the study book.

Form four small groups. Assign each group a "fundamental characteristic" of Christianity as outlined in the section, "Four Characteristics of Christianity." Each group should review the section of the text that relates to the topic and decide whether or not this issue is essential to Christian unity and why:

- Incarnation
- Formation of community
- God-inspired authoritative writings
- Relationship to secular government

When the groups have had time to work, invite a spokesperson from each group to list its topic under the appropriate heading (Essential or Nonessential) and explain the group's reasoning.

Now, call out the following issues, and ask the group to vote on whether the topic is essential or nonessential to Christian unity and record the issue in the appropriate column. For the sake of this exercise, let a simple voice vote make the decision. If there is broad disagreement among the group, invite one or two people to speak to their choice.

- Baptism (adult or infant)
- Belief in God
- Bible as fact
- Capital punishment
- Communion
- Divinity of Jesus
- Divorce
- Doctrine of the Holy Spirit
- End-of-life decisions
- Missionary service
- Old Testament in the Bible
- Ordination of homosexuals
- Ordination of women
- Original sin
- Predestination
- Racism
- Reality of the Resurrection
- Reproductive issues
- Sexual relationships
- Slavery
- Worship styles
- Other topics: invite group members to suggest additional topics

Wrapping Up

Practice

Ask participants to reflect on the session question: "Why do Christians disagree about so many things?"

In pairs, have each participant, in turn, pose/answer the session question. Prompt pairs to switch roles when half of the allotted time has passed. Those posing the question should engage in active listening, to be prepared to share what they have heard when the group gathers again.

After all of the participants have had an opportunity to ask and answer the question, gather the group and invite people to share what they heard.

Closing

Invite participants to reflect on the lessons learned throughout the study, and to share ways in which their lives of faith have been affected by participating in the study.

Closing Prayer

Lord of all, we ask first to be one in you. Help us to be humble in confessing our failures and in seeking deeper love for you and for one another. In all things, help us to rely on your grace to guide and open our hearts to live in unity. Amen.

CPSIA information can be obtained
at www.ICGtesting.com
Printed in the USA
LVHW031327290721
693988LV00003B/86

9 781501 803352